This is what you should do;
love the Earth and sun and the animals.

Walt Whitman

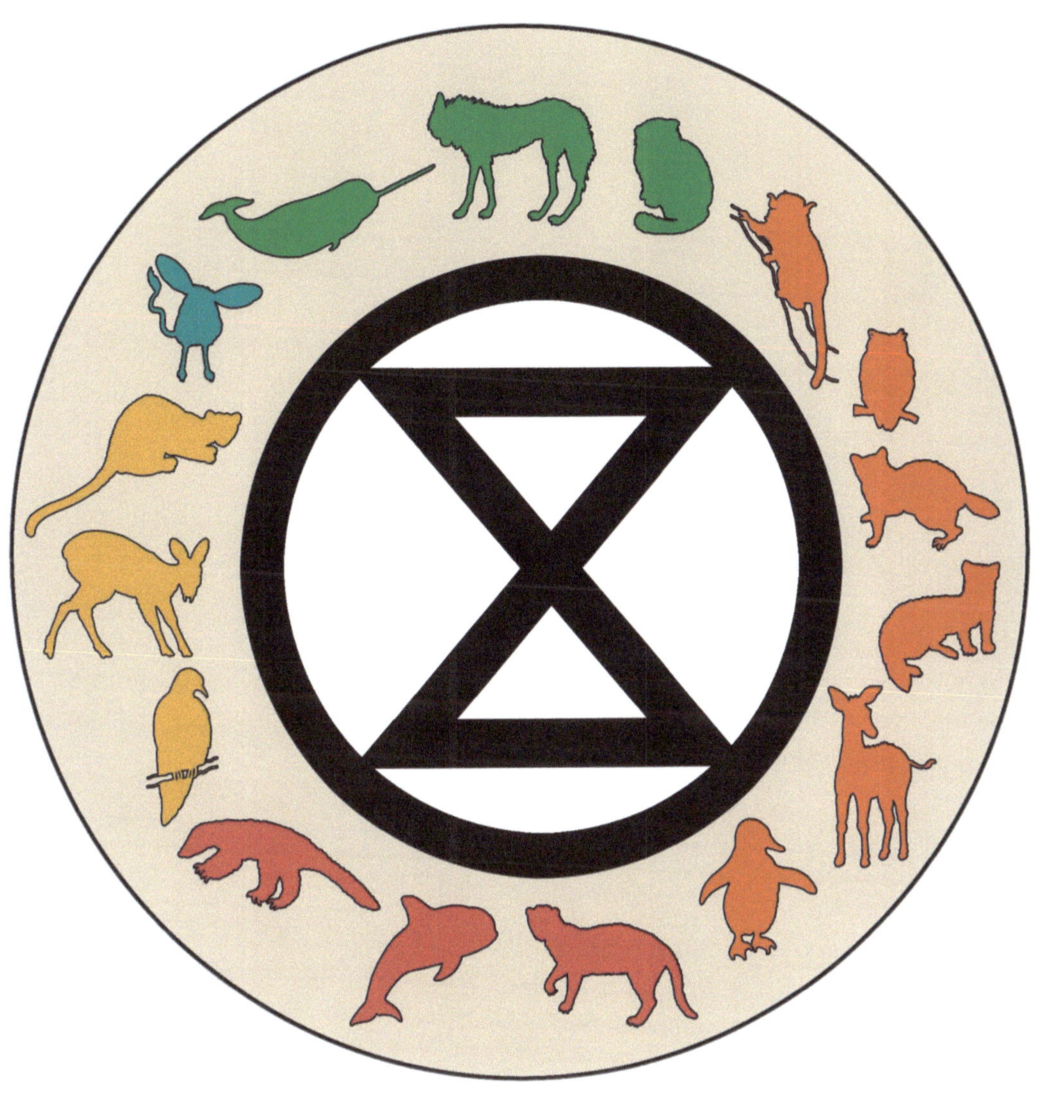

This symbol represents extinction. The circle signifies the planet, while the hourglass inside serves as a warning that time is rapidly running out for many species. This ongoing process of destruction is being caused by the impact of human activity. Within the next few decades approximately 50% of all species that now exist will have become extinct.

EXTINCTION IS FOREVER

The map which follows shows where in the world the animals featured in this coloring book are located. Also shown, using the official color code, is the status of each animal on the **Endangered Species List.** This ranges from least concern to critically endangered. Also included are 16 colored illustrations of the main animals along with descriptions, interesting facts and other species included on that page. If you'd like more information, **wikipedia** is a good place to start!

Founded in 1991 by Dr. Jane Goodall, *Jane Goodall's Roots & Shoots* is a youth service program for young people of all ages. Their mission is to foster respect and compassion for all living things, to promote understanding of all cultures and beliefs, and to inspire each individual to take action to make the world a better place for people, other animals, and the environment.

Below are some great links to learning more about our animals and earth and what we can do to help!

https://www.rootsandshoots.org/user/139989/tos?destination=homepage

http://kids.nationalgeographic.com/explore/nature/mission-animal-rescue/

http://www.animalfactguide.com/animal-facts/

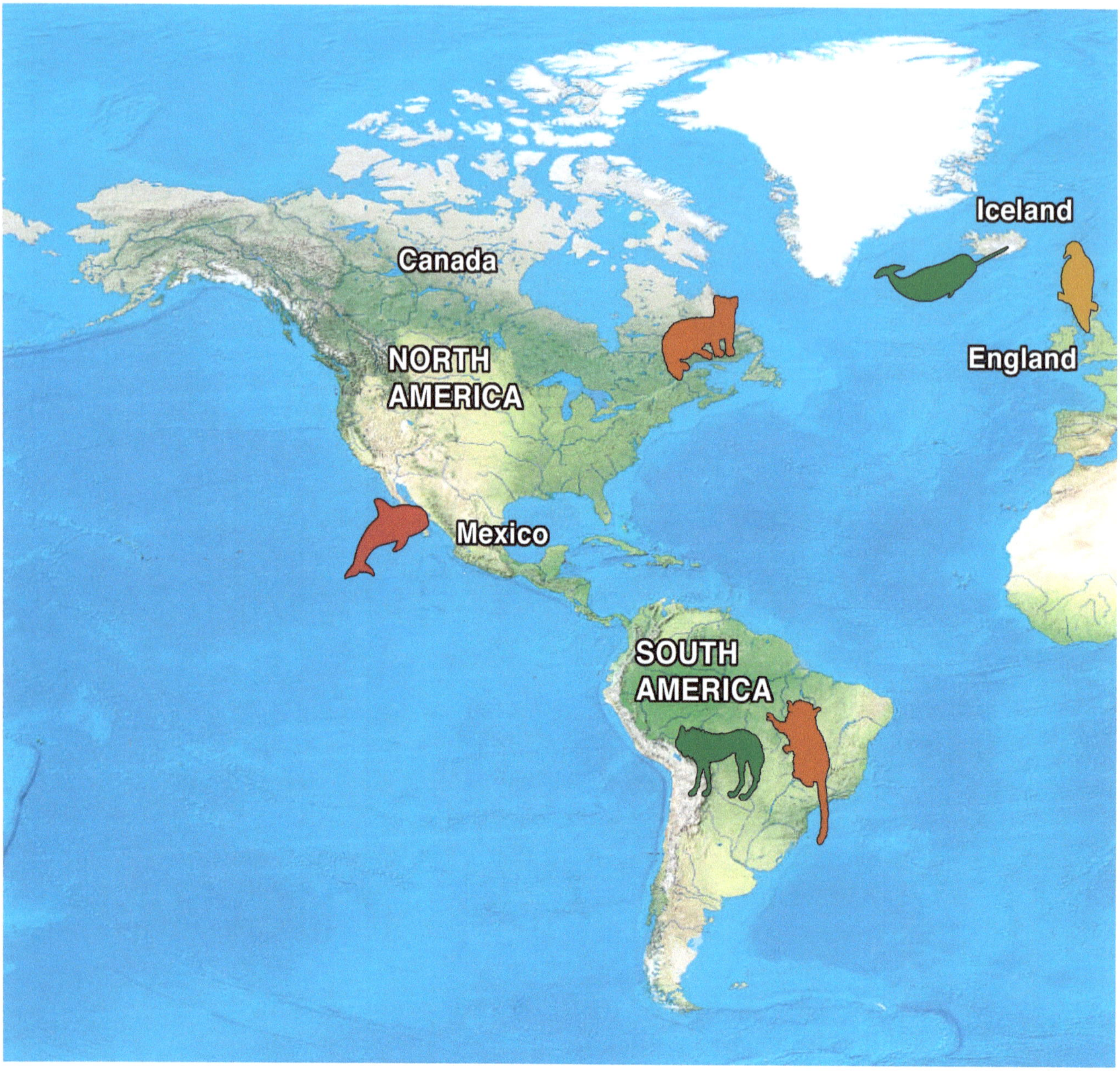

Iceland

Canada

England

NORTH
AMERICA

Mexico

SOUTH
AMERICA

Endangered Animals

LEAST CONCERN

Long Eared Jerboa

NEAR THREATENED

Pallas's Cat
Maned Wolf
Narwhal

VULNERABLE

Fossa
Siberian Musk Deer
European Turtle Dove

Around The World

ENDANGERED

Okapi
Blakiston's Fish Owl
Pied Tamarin
Yellow-Eyed Penguin
Eastern Quoll
Newfoundland Pine Marten

CRITICALLY ENDANGERED

Vaquita
Chinese Pangolin
Malabar Large Spotted Civet

 **Malabar Large Spotted Civet**

The Malabar Large Spotted Civet is one of the world's rarest species. It is believed to be endemic to the Western Ghats of southern India inhabiting the forests and richly wooded lowland. With the elimination of its habitat, the Malabar Large Spotted Civet population declined drastically. By the 1960s, the species was thought to be extinct. However, members of the species were found in the late 1980s, and some isolated groups are still known to exist. Although most civets resemble spotted, long-nosed cats, the Malabar Civets are more dog-like in appearance, with long legs and rather canine heads and muzzles. One reason for the disappearance of the Malabar Civet is the use of "civet musk" in the manufacture of perfumes. The largest threat to the species, however, is the deforestation of its original habitat in the Western Ghats, which forces the population into tiny isolated areas.

Indian Star Tortoise 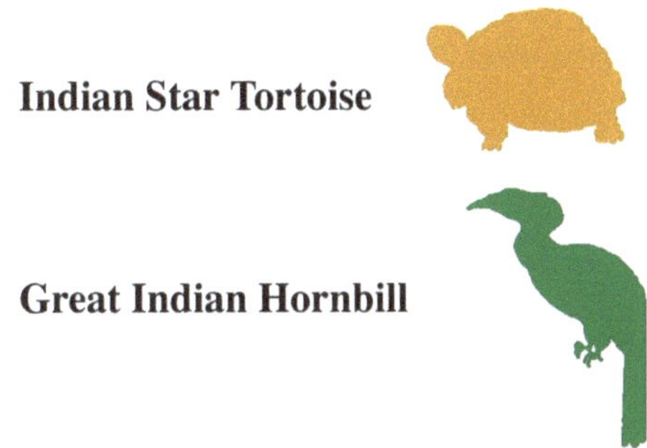

Great Indian Hornbill

 LEAST CONCERN　　 NEAR THREATENED　　 VULNERABLE　　 ENDANGERED　　 CRITICALLY ENDANGERED

 **Okapi**

Sometimes called forest giraffes, this elusive animal is found in small pockets of tropical mountain forest in central Africa. Okapis have the body of a horse and striped legs like a zebra. The animals are about eight feet long and six and a half feet high at the shoulder. Their weight ranges from 465 to 550 pounds. The Okapi is the giraffe's only living relative and shares some features such as elongated necks, long dark tongues and the males have small horns. Okapis are herbivores, meaning plant eating, and feed on tree leaves, grass, ferns, fruit and fungi. Major threats to these shy elusive animals include habitat loss due to logging and human settlement as well as illegal poaching. The rate of decline is estimated to have exceeded 50% over 24 years, based on figures from surveys in the Okapi Wildlife Reserve. Okapis have been protected by law in the Democratic Republic of Congo (formally Zaire) since 1933.

 LEAST CONCERN    NEAR THREATENED    VULNERABLE    ENDANGERED   CRITICALLY ENDANGERED

 ## Vaquita

The Vaquita, which means *little cow* in Spanish, is a rare species of porpoise endemic to the Northern part of the Gulf of California. This porpoise is the world's smallest cetacean and most endangered marine animal. The Vaquita has a gray body with a pale gray or white belly and a dark patch around its eye and lips. Their weight tops out at 120 lbs and its life cycle is around twenty years. Approximately 30 remain as their population is decreasing at an astonishing rate. The rapidfall of the population is a direct result of illegal trade in an endangered fish species, the Totoaba, which is caught in nets that entangle Vaquitas. These animals represent more, proportionally, of the tree of life than other species, meaning they are top priority for conservation campaigns.

Axolotl

Kemp's Ridley

 Newfoundland Pine Marten

The Newfoundland Pine Marten is a native and distinct subspecies of the american marten found only on the island of Newfoundland. The Marten is about the size of a small house cat with a long slender body. Its fur is also dark brown with a yellow patch at the throat. These animals prefer thick dark woods with a dense canopy as their habitat. They feed on small prey, mostly meadow voles. The females give birth in April to one to five kits in dens underground and sometimes on steep slopes. In Newfoundland the natural predators of the Martens include lynx, owls and red fox. Habitat loss, rabbit snares, accidental trapping, disease and the possible scarcity of food are also threats to the Marten population. The Marten was listed as endangered in 2001 and has been protected since 1934, however the population still declines.

Snowy Owl

Caribou

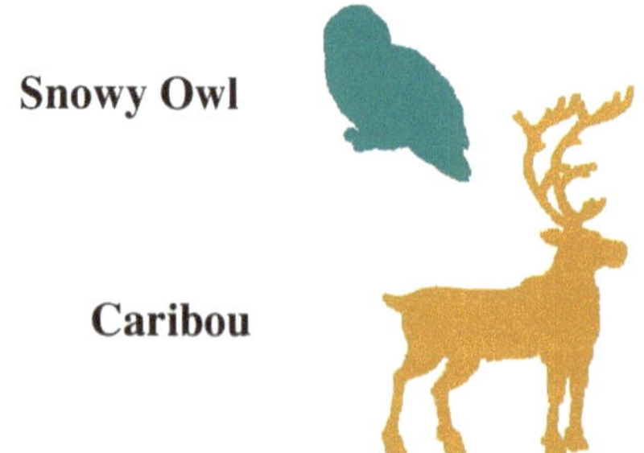

● Narwhal

The Narwhal, the unicorn of the sea, is a medium sized whale and lives in arctic waters. Male bulls can weigh nearly two tons with bodies up to sixteen feet long. The spiraled tusk of the Narwhal is actually a tooth that grows from a hole in the upper lip and can be up to ten feet long. It contains millions of tiny holes that act as a sensor for the whale. Narwhals feed in deep bays and inlets where they find a good supply of arctic cod, squid, and other food such as flatfish and shrimp. Limited Data suggests females only have one calf every three years. The calves measure five feet and can weigh 180 lbs at birth. They stay with their mother for almost two years. Oil and gas development as well as climate change pose threats to Narwhals. Like polar bears, the Narwhal depends on sea ice for its existence.

Atlantic Puffin 

Walrus

 LEAST CONCERN  NEAR THREATENED  VULNERABLE  ENDANGERED  CRITICALLY ENDANGERED

 **Turtle Dove**

The small, delicate Turtle Dove is slightly larger than a black-bird. It has dark black and chestnut upper parts with a white belly and pink breast. Throughout history the Turtle Dove has been a symbol of love and peace. It is Britain's only migratory bird. The species departs Europe in September to winter in Africa. It has been included here due to the rapid decline of it's breeding population by an alarming 91% in the last 10 years. Turtle Doves mate for life. They like to nest in thick hedgerows and only two eggs are laid in each clutch. Until recently it was usual for Doves to have three nesting attempts each summer. Today the children of Britain will go silent when singing the twelve days of Christmas and come to the part of "two Turtle Doves" to call attention to their plight. The RSPB's Operation Turtle Dove is working hard to reverse the Dove's decline in the UK. These declines are driven by many factorsincluding loss of foraging and nesting sites as well as disease and hunting along their migration path.

Red Squirrel

European Hedgehog

 **Siberian Musk Deer**

The Siberian Musk deer has a face similar to a kangaroo and vampire like fangs. They are found in the forests of Siberia as well Mongolia and parts of China and Korea. This shy and timid species is generally solitary. It feeds at dusk and dawn on leaves, flowers, grasses and lichen. Males grow the fangs instead of antlers. The older the deer, the longer the fangs. Males excrete a musk odor to attract the does. Unfortunately the Musk scent also attracts humans as it is used in the making of perfumes and medicines. This is the main reason for their declining numbers.

Russian Des 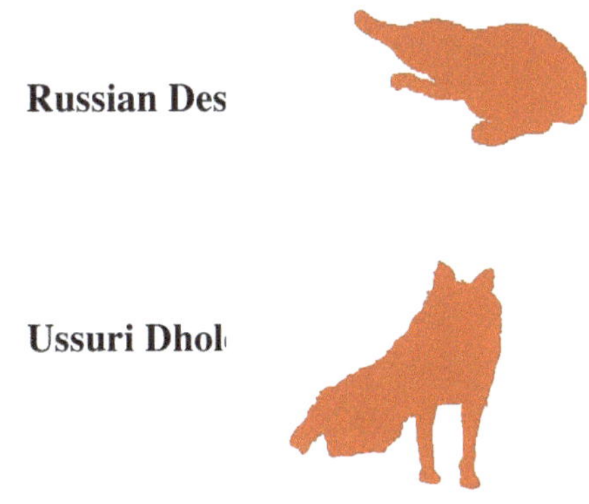

Ussuri Dhol

 **Pied Tamarin**

The Pied Tamarin is a primate of small size and lives in the Brazilian rainforest of South America. They are thought to be the most threatened primates of this region. Their height is a mere 7 to 12 inches and weight is 0.5 to 2 pounds. They feed on nectar, frogs, lizards, eggs and insects. Pied Tamarins live in troops of 3 to 15. They rest in trees and forage for food during the day. Pied Tamarins are threatened primarily by habitat loss and only occupy a small area in Brazil.

Amazonian Manatee

 LEAST CONCERN  NEAR THREATENED  VULNERABLE  ENDANGERED  CRITICALLY ENDANGERED

 **Maned Wolf**

The Maned Wolf is the largest member of the dog family in South America. The animal looks like a fox, is called a wolf, and is closely related to neither. The Maned Wolf's fox-like characteristics and thin long legs have earned it the nickname of "fox on stilts." These gentle and timid wolves are solitary by nature. Only during the breeding season would you generally see more than one at a time. The Maned Wolf is monogamous meaning they only take one mate for life. The female gives birth to four to five cubs in her den. The Maned Wolf is omnivorous, eating a combination of fruits, vegetables and meat. It preys on small birds, rodents and frogs, and favors fruits such as bananas, apples and avocados. They have what is called a roar-bark. The sound is mostly used by mates to communicate with each other over long distances. When threatened, the thick mane hairs stand erect, making it appear larger. In addition to habitat loss, the species is subject to other serious threats, including road kills, direct persecution by humans, and disease due to contact with domestic animals.

Pygmy Three-toed Sloth

Baird's Tapir

 LEAST CONCERN    NEAR THREATENED    VULNERABLE    ENDANGERED    CRITICALLY ENDANGERED

Chinese Pangolin

Pangolins, also known as scaly anteaters, are unique animals that are covered in hard scales. There are eight types, four of which live in Asia and four in Africa. Their name pangolinis derived from the Malay word which loosely translates to "*something that rolls up*." This is what they do when threatened to protect themselves. They do not have teeth but instead long sticky tongues that are used to feed on insects. Pangolins are solitary, nocturnal and very secretive, therefore many mysteries remain about their behavior. The female give birth to one offspring. The baby rides on it's mother's tail and will stay with her until two years of age. The biggest threat to all Pangolin species is illegal hunting for human consumption. Their scales are widely used in traditional Chinese medicines. Researchers warned last year that the Chinese Pangolin is in danger of being "eaten to extinction" because of huge demand.

Ili Pika

Red Panda

 ### Eastern Quoll

The Eastern Quoll is a carnivorous (meat eating) marsupial. Marsupial animals carry their young in a pouch. Marsupials are only found in Australia and the Americas. The quoll is about the size of a small cat. They have thick fur with white spots that cover the body but in the eastern quoll not the furry tail. Their color can be fawn, brown or black. The eastern quoll tends to live alone, foraging mainly on beetle larvae and grubs as well as small mammals such as mice, birds, lizards and snakes. The females can give birth to thirty young but there is only room for six in her pouch. They remain there for two months and then will be carried on their mother's back for another six weeks. Quolls are threatened by the spread of poisonous cane toads as well as dogs, collision with vehicles, and illegal poisoning. The species is wholly protected by law.

Regent Honey Eater

Abbott's Booby

Red-Bellied Short Necked Turtle

 LEAST CONCERN  NEAR THREATENED  VULNERABLE  ENDANGERED  CRITICALLY ENDANGERED

 ### Yellow Eyed Penguin

The Yellow Eyed Penguin is one of the most endangered of all Penguin species. They are found on the south island of New Zealand. As their common name suggests they have yellow eyes, accented by the yellow band that runs from the eyes to the back of the head. Unlike most Penguins that breed in colonies, yellow-eyed penguins are the least social and breed in forests. Pairs mate for life and make their nests of twigs near the base of trees. They lay 2 eggs and both help to feed the chicks. Today, the Yellow-Eyed Penguin has an estimated wild population of less than 4,000 individuals. It is now the rarest Penguin in the world due to deforestation and the introduction of mammalian predators.

West Coast Green Gecko 

 Blakiston's Fish Owl

The Blakiston's Fish Owl is the largest living species of owl. It's found only in wooded areas in the east of Japan's second-largest island, Hokkaido, and in small areas in adjacent Russiaand China. The Blakiston's Fish Owl's nickname means *"philosopher in the wood."* Blakiston's fish owl have a wingspan that can reach just over six feet and height up to 28 inches. The facial disc is greyish with very long ear tufts. The Blakiston's Fish Owl feeds on a variety of aquatic prey including pike, catfish, trout and salmon. These owls prefer nesting in hollow tree cavities. Females lay one to three eggs. The males provide food for the incubating female and later the nestlings. The Blakiston's Fish Owl is endangered due to the widespread loss of riverine forest and through increasing development. The current population in Japan is 100 to 150 birds.

 ### Long-Eared Jerboa

The Long-Eared Jerboa, a mysterious mouse like creature, can be found in the Gobi desert of Mongolia and north western China. This species is distinguished from other Jerboas by its enormous ears, which are three times larger than its head. Their legs resemble that of a kangaroo and are used for hopping. They are nocturnal and spend hours of daylight in underground burrows sleeping. The species is thought to be declining as a result of human disturbance of it's habitat.

Reed Parrotbill

Bactrian Camel

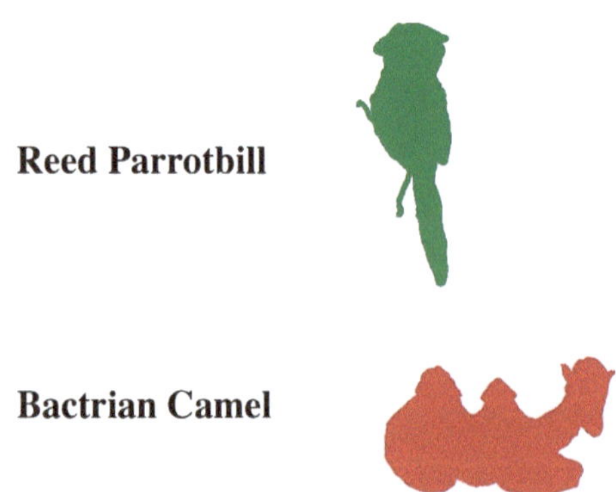

 LEAST CONCERN  NEAR THREATENED  VULNERABLE  ENDANGERED  CRITICALLY ENDANGERED

● Fossa

The Fossa is the largest meat eating mammal on the island of Madagascar. They can reach nearly six feet in length, with half of that due to their long tails. They are a cross between a dog, cat and mongoose. Members of this family are thought to have descended from mongoose-like ancestors that colonized Madagascar about 20 million years ago. They have slender bodies, muscular limbs, and short, reddish-brown coats. They are agile tree climbers and feed on small mammals including fish, lizards, birds, frogs, and insects. The female Fossa gives birth to 2 – 6 cubs. They remain dependent on their mother for over a year. The Fossa is endangered due to habitat loss. Less than ten percent of Madagascar's original intact forest cover, the fossa's only home, remains today.

Panther Chameleon

Grey Mouse Lemur

 LEAST CONCERN    NEAR THREATENED    VULNERABLE    ENDANGERED    CRITICALLY ENDANGERED

Pallas's cat

The Pallas's cat is about the size of a domestic house cat although may appears larger due to their stout stature and thick coat of fur. They have short ears and round pupils unlike house cats that have vertical pupils. Pallas's cats are best adapted to cold arid environments in rocky country at fairly high elevations. They make their dens in caves and crevices. The cat is a solitary creature and feeds on Pika and other rodents. The two primary threats concerning the Pallas's cat are the hunting of the cat for it's fur and the poisoning of it's primary food source.

Himalyan Monal

Four-horned Antelope

We are all connected in the web of life. Animals and plants rely on each other to survive. If the web forms a hole due to the loss of a species, it becomes fragile and more holes start to form until the web is left in fragments. This is why preserving habitat and protecting endangered species is very important! Do your part and be a defender of wildlife!

This book is dedicated to my grandchildren Zoe and Zander, and all the children of the earth. Nature is truly a magnificent teacher!

Drawing by Zoe Olson age 8

Pledge by Cherl Crews. Created for the 40th anniversary of Earth Day by students from Hearthstone School and Belle Meade School.

"When we try to pick out anything by itself, we find it hitched to everything else in the universe."

John Muir

MALABAR LARGE SPOTTED CIVET   India

OKAPI Africa

VAQUITA Mexico

NEWFOUNDLAND PINE MARTEN Canada

NARWHAL Iceland

EUROPEAN TURTLE DOVE England

SIBERIAN MUSK DEER Russia

PIED TAMARIN Amazon Rainforest

MANED WOLF South America

PANGOLIN China

EASTERN QUOLL Australia

YELLOW EYED PENGUIN New Zealand

BLAKISTON'S FISH OWL   Japan

LONG EARED JERBOA Mongolia

FOSSA Madagascar

PALLAS'S CAT Nepal

www.ingramcontent.com/pod-product-compliance
Lightning Source LLC
Chambersburg PA
CBHW040137240726
48664CB00002B/510